Michael Bittner, Fourth Grade, Unalaska School

"The editors have put together a beautiful children's book on our ferry system. It's written by children for children and shows a different concept of this vital system to Alaska that all ages can enjoy. Refreshing!"

Captian Robert M. Johnson,
Master of *M/V MATANUSKA*

"Delightful! It's so good to see our students in print as the experts they are on a subject so important and fascinating to them. The book is an excellent incentive for budding young Alaskan authors."

Marsha Buck, Principal,
Wonder Park Elementary, Anchorage

"This delightful book is full of life and fun and information as it presents fascinating facts and stories about Alaskan ferries. Because it speaks through the words and pictures of young authors and illustrators, it sparks its readers' own desires to write creatively. This book truly belongs in every elementary classroom and library."

Katheryn E. White, former elementary administrator in Highline School District, Seattle, and author of children's literature

ALASKAN FERRY TALES FOR CHILDREN

Stories, Poems, Artwork and Anecdotes Collected from Children in Alaska

Collected and edited by
Marilyn Cochran Mosley, Ed.D.
Joyce Delbridge
Patricia Evans

Consulting Art Editor and Book Design:
Marilyn Foulkes, Peacock Productions

JMP Productions, Inc.
Vashon Island, Washington

Hai Han Ye, Age 13, Whittier School

A special note of appreciation goes to the Alaska Marine Highway, State of Alaska, Department of Transportation and Public Facilities, and to Linda S. Mickle, Reservation Specialist and Customer Services for the Alaska Marine Highway.

We also wish to express our appreciation to the teachers who worked with their students to prepare material for the Ferry Tales Contest, and to the Alaska Marine Highways employees who agreed to be interviewed.

Library of Congress: 89-080605

ISBN: 0-9614850-3-5

Cover Illustration by:
Daniel Gaston
Age 7, Correspondence (Juneau)

Printed by Snohomish Publishing Company Inc.

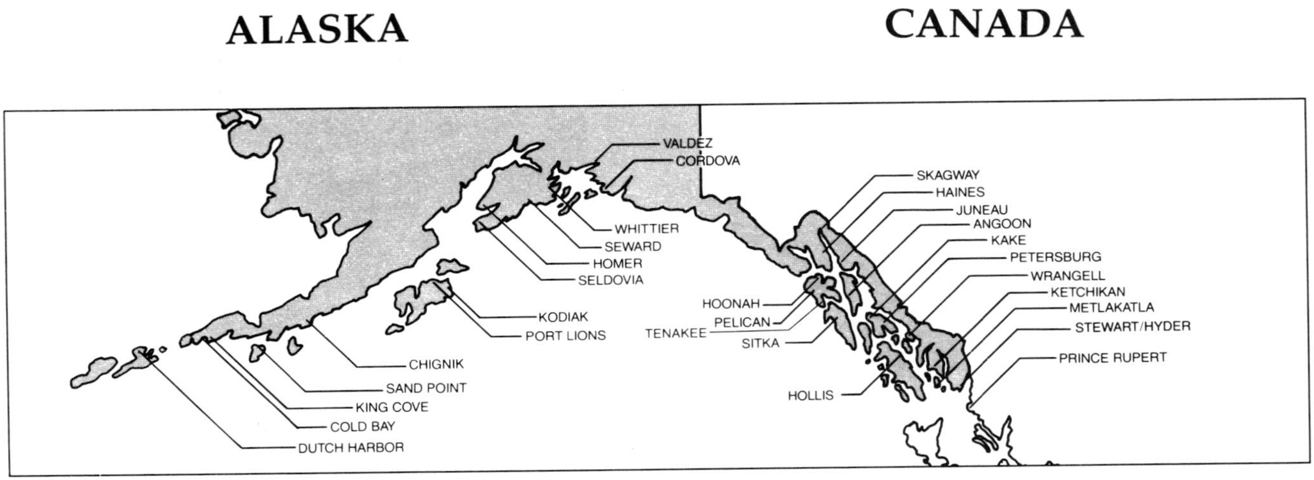

The Alaska Marine Highway

The Alaskan Marine Highway

Have you ever heard of traveling on a highway in a boat? That is just what over 350,000 people did last year. They climbed aboard one of the nine vessels belonging to the Alaska Marine Highway System and traveled from Dutch Harbor to Kodiak, Cordova, and Valdez, from Seattle and Prince Rupert to Skagway, and points in between.

Look at the map on the opposite page. Many of the towns along Alaska's long coast line are water bound. There are no roads to connect them with the outside world so these towns depend on ferries for transportation and supplies. By traveling on ferries, people can go to bigger towns to shop, to attend sports events, to conduct business, and to socialize. As you can easily see, ferries are important in the life of people in Alaska.

The children who wrote this book are familiar with the wonderful sights that can be seen from their ferries. They see great chunks of ice fall from the glaciers and float in the ice cold water. They see whales and seals and other marine animals and watch bears fishing for salmon in spawning season. Perhaps one day you will be able to visit this beautiful, wild land for yourself. We invite you to come aboard and join our voyage with Jeremy Andrews as your host.

The Editors

TABLE OF CONTENTS

About Being the Ferry

I travel on the route of Southeast
While doing a slow walk.
I stop at place and place
To see new faces, old friends.
I feel safe when at rest at a dock.
Russell Dalton

I see with the eyes of my watch.
He tells me where sharp rocks or submerged icebergs are.
Jennifer Shandy

My long tongue extends out, slowly,
Slowly down go the cars.
Going, down, down, down. And GULP!
I close my mouth, move on.
At the next port, I burp some up.
Ken Brown

My engine pumps the fuel through which I live.
The heart-center.
Brindle Budd

Fuel is the glucose for my energy.
Kamal Lindoff

The bridge is the thinking center.
Here to react to logs, danger,
Controlled by computers and men.
Roy Hill

The brain is the main control of the whole,
Giving commands, giving directions,
Telling the wheel, telling the rudder.
Robert Sharclane

My legs propel. I push fast. I move slow,
From starboard to port, port to starboard,
In calm or rough waters.
Gus Mills

My home can be as rough or as uncomfortable as a bed of sharp stones,
Or my bed may be as smooth as a real water bed.
Corinna Quilliam

I transport people, some sick, some not,
Through dark nights, gloomy days, heavy seas, sunshine.
Gretchen Oliver

I travel on the route of Alaska Marine Highway
While doing a slow walk.
I stop at place to place
To see new faces, old friends.

The Class of '93
Sixth Grade
Jetta Budd, Teacher
Hoonah Public Schools

J.P. Stelzer, Age 8, Third Grade, Chiniak School

On February 29, I went aboard the *Matanuska* for a ferry ride from Haines to Skagway to interview the Captain, Bob Johnson, and the Chief Engineer. I traveled as the guest of the captain, and later that night, was his guest for dinner.

Jeremy Andrews
Age 13, Eighth Grade
Klukwan School

Jeremy Andrews

Marine Highway

What's a marine highway?
traveling by boat
eating ice cream
meeting new people
playing video games
going to the gift shop
sleeping in the solarium
That's a marine highway.

Amy Richardson
Age 13, Seventh Grade
Hoonah Elementary School

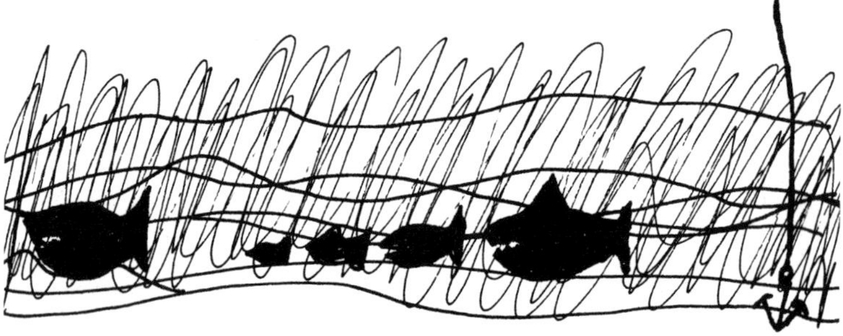

Robby Palagyi
Age7, Second Grade
McNeil Canyon School (Homer)

Ol' Brake Light

After driving 22 miles from Klukwan to the Haines Ferry Terminal, we finally got onto the ferry. We were headed for the Southeast Alaska Fine Arts Camp. We covered our seats with blankets, as we had a smelly Springer Spaniel with us. We turned off the lights, went upstairs to the forward lounge, and rolled out our sleeping bags.

A voice boomed over the loud speaker. "Will Bob Andrews please come to the purser's desk?" My father went to the desk. Ellen Searby, a ferry worker, told him his brake lights were on. He was sure he had turned them off, but, sure enough, after going down to check, the brake lights were on. He opened the front door and was greeted by our dog, Mike, who had been sleeping on the brake. We propped up the brake with a couple of blankets so even if he decided to sleep on it again, it wouldn't move.

About two weeks later, we saw Ellen Searby again, and she asked, "How's Ol' Brake Light?"

Jeremy Andrews
Age 12, Seventh Grade
Klukwan School

(Editor's Note: On Alaskan ferries, animals must be kept in cars or in cages on the car deck. Passengers are not allowed to stay on the car deck but are provided time to check their pets, and give them a walk at regular intervals during the trip.)

The Wet Surprise

The Alaskan Ferry is one way to get close to nature. But sometimes you can get a little bit too close. One day my mom and I went on the ferry. I was on the first floor of the ferry. All of a sudden a gigantic whale jumped out of the water. SPLASH**?? ***???? The whale got me so wet! I ran into our room and said, "Mom, Mom, I just saw a real whale! And it got me this wet." The end.

Jeremy Stone
Age 10, Third Grade
Chiniak School

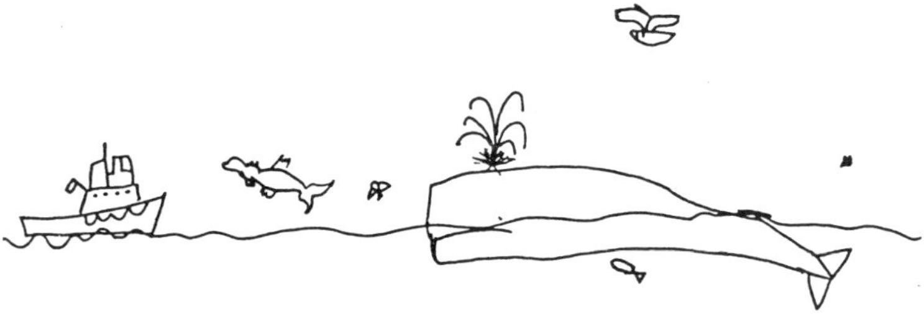

Jacob de Leon, Age 10, Third Grade, Unalaska School

A Shark Bited the Ferry

A shark bited the ferry and it made a hole in the ferry but the men put something there so no more water came in. There were men that served food. Lots of people were on it that I didn't know but Harriett was on it and Scott was on it. That's all.

Jaime Stanford
Age 5, Kindergarten
Klukwan School

The Ferry Has Cars

The ferry has cars and
compartments and
restaurants and plants
and moms and dads and
kids and flowers and
nurses.

Danielle Ludwigsen
Age 6, First Grade
Holy Name School (Ketchikan)

Becky Marie Hale, Age 11, Fifth Grade, Rowan Bay School

Aaron Hotch, Age 7, Second Grade, Klukwan School

The primary role a ferry captain has is to insure the safety of the vessel, the crew, and the passengers. He is in charge of all the departments, like the Steward's Department, the Engineer's Department, the Purser's Department. He also is in charge of navigation, like going through the narrows, docking, or in rough weather. On calm days, other people may take over.

Jeremy

Katie Ann Rooney, Third Grade, Unalaska School

What We See

When we ride the ferry here is what we see:

A grayish-black porpoise like a missile
A sea lion, belly-flopping into the waves
Flocks of ducks flying close to the water on fast wings
A soaring eagle - watching squirming yellowish reddish fish
Killer whales - inky, milky - leaping
Humpback whales - diving into the water
Smooth curious seal with small sad eyes
Otter doing a backfloat - cracking clams in the drifting seaweed
A shark - hunting - killing - fin up
An ambling bear
A bounding, springing deer
Ravens - smart, dark as night - screeching
Seagulls - soaring, following in our wake.

Fourth Grade Class
Claudia McConnell, Teacher
Hoonah Elementary School

The Crew of the *Taku*

On the *Taku*, there is a crew of thirty people. They work twelve hours a day straight. But of course they have coffee breaks and lunch breaks. They get about fifteen dollars an hour and they work two weeks then they have two weeks off. If you want to be a worker on the ferry you have to have a Coast Guard License and you have to take an important test. Before you take the test you must study very hard for it. Sometimes a person may study for a year or more. All of the workers on the ferry must also have Life Boat Training. Not all ferries have exactly thirty workers. The bigger ones have more and the smaller ones have less. So whenever you go on the ferry, there are highly trained workers to serve you.

Deanna L. King
Age 13, Eighth Grade
Klukwan School

Shark

Once a ferry was drifting on the water and a shark came and almost pulled off a man.

Colette Thompson
Age 7, First Grade
Holy Name School (Ketchikan)

Erik Reimnitz, Age 12, Seventh Grade, McMurray Middle School, (Vashon Island, Washington)

The Curse of the *Flying Dutchman*

Once upon a time there was a ship called the *Flying Dutchman*. The captain was Vanderdecker. He was very fond of speeding around making money. Back then faster was better. It's like truck driving today. If you're not moving you're not making any money.

One day, the *Flying Dutchman* was caught in a rough storm. They were trying to get to a port down somewhere in the area of Cape of Good Hope. They had a choice to either go around, which would be much calmer, or take a way through rocks and reefs near the shore which would be faster. Vanderdecker made the fatal choice, and took the one near the shore. A man stood up to him but was killed and supposedly thrown overboard.

When they got to Cape of Good Hope, a ghost appeared on the deck of the ship. It was seen many times before around that area. The ghost put a curse on the captain. He must keep sailing or die with a sword in his back. The other part of the curse was that if any other ship was to ever see the *Flying Dutchman* something bad would happen to it.

About ten years ago the *Taku's* crew was doing their thing, working, watching for hidden dangers, and plotting the course for the ferry. A man on watch in the early morning saw a ship float out of the fog - it was the *Flying Dutchman!* Some of the other crew members saw it also and were afraid of what might happen to them. They knew in their bones that it wasn't a cloud or their imagination.

Donald S. Hotch, Jr., Age 12, Seventh Grade, Klukwan School

Josh P. Batchelor, Age 12, Sixth Grade, Floyd Dryden Middle School (Juneau)

To become a ferry captain, there are many things you have to do. Just to qualify, you need a certain amount of sea time, and you have to have graduated from Radar School. Then you can get the 3rd Mates License. After a year, you can get a 2nd Mates License. After another year, you can get a Chief's License, and then finally, you can earn your Master's License, meaning you're a captain. Actually, it's not that simple. To become a Master, you have to have a Pilotage License for the areas your ship travels through, and a federal license.

Jeremy

Tracy Wallace
Age 12, Sixth Grade
Floyd Dryden Middle School (Juneau)

Fish, Big Mountains and Lots of Water

On Alaska's ferries you can see pretty things like seals, fish, big mountains and lots of water. You can take your boat and camper or car with you TOO.

David B. Lilly
Age 5, Kindergarten
Taku Elementary School (Anchorage)

David B. Lilly
Age 5, Kindergarten
Taku Elementary School (Anchorage)

ROUND TRIP

Ferry boat
Boat ride
Ride waves
Wave to friends
Friendship
Ship to dock
Docking vibration
Vibrating Sounds
Sounds of arcade games
Games of cards
Card deck
Deck hands
Hands on luggage
Luggage cart
Carting people
People in Alaska
Alaska ferry
Ferry boat.

Class of '93
Sixth Grade
Jetta Budd, Teacher
Hoonah Elementary School

Luke Randall, Age 6, First Grade, Correspondence (Seal Bay)

Some interesting things have happened to Captain Johnson. For instance, he has been charged by a whale. Well, actually the whale had been wounded by killer whales, and was trying to get away. He has also seen St. Elmo's Fire, where during the night, the wires and railings glowed. Sometimes while he pilots through Puget Sound, nuclear submarines surface around him, or send up a periscope.

Jeremy

Captain Johnson

The Ferry is Fun

On the ferry I can see water and mountains and fish.
I can hear whistles the captain makes,
I can taste ice cream and yogurt and
hot dogs,
I can smell fish and water and gas,
I can feel air.
The ferry is fun.

Lucas Harrington
Second Grade
Holy Name School (Ketchikan)

Taste, Smell, Feel, See

On the ferry I can taste french fries and ice
cream.
I can smell diesel oil,
I can feel the waves,
The ferry is beautiful.

Erin Eddy
Age 8, Second Grade
Holy Name School (Ketchikan)

Michelle Dilbeck, Age 11, Sixth Grade, Floyd Dryden Middle School (Juneau)

From Seattle to Ketchikan

I went on the *Malaspina* coming home from my Christmas vacation. I went from Seattle to Ketchikan, Alaska. The engine broke down and had to turn back when we were just about to Ketchikan.

I met many girls on the ferry. I think it is fun because you can play games and eat good food. We watched Alaska Marine Highway shows. We saw eagles in the trees and saw porpoises and dolphins. We also saw some black bears on the beach.

We were two days late getting into Ketchikan.

Erik Grove
Age 10, Fourth Grade
Rowan Bay School

What I Can Do

I get upon the ferry,
And then what I can do,
Is go inside and take a ride
And eat a burger too.

Ezra Sbonek
Age 7, First Grade
Correspondence (Point Baker)

On the Ferry, My Brother and Me

Rolling on the dark blue sea,
On the ferry, my brother and me,
I see a fish jumping around,
Then gaze at the sky without a sound.

A puffin flutters and flies on by,
A small black speck on the bright, blue sky.
The snow on the mountains reflect the sun,
And I ask my brother if he's having fun.

I soon see the place where we're going to dock,
After such a long ride it was quite a shock.
And now that I've seen, these great
Alaskan scenes, I think I'll go
Home and eat some pork and beans.

Amy Darling
Age 9, Fourth Grade
Tracyton Elementary (Silverdale, Washington)

Lisa Larson, Age 6, First Grade, Rowan Bay School

Danny Mathew Subramanian, Age 12, Sixth Grade, Klukwan School

When asked if he (the captain) could start over, would he choose the same career, he gives a definite,"yes." He enjoys the work he does, and doesn't care for working on the land. He comes from a long line of seafarers, so it was the natural job for him to choose.

Jeremy

Ella Hotch, Age 7, First Grade, Klukwan School

My First Time on the Ferry

My first time on the ferry was fun. But when my brother left me it was scary.

When I found out I told my mom. My mom got mad at my brother and now he has to stay with me close to my mom. My brother took me to the videos.

It was fun. Once we passed my best friend. My brother got mad because I was talking to her too long. So we ended up by the videos again. It was boring because we went to the videos so much.

And then we went outside and my brother scared me. And then we went to the money cashier. My brother had a lot.

And then we went to the candy machine with all his money. It was yummy. I had Twix and Matt had the Three Musketeers.

Then we were pulled into the harbor. I was mad because I like it on the ferry.

Bethany Joy Davidson
Age 7, Second Grade
Klukwan School

Bethany Joy Davidson, Age 7, Second Grade, Klukwan School

Tim Botz, Age 6, First Grade, Chiniak School

Being a ferry captain also has some good benefits. For one thing, it has a really good retirement program. It also has great living conditions, involving a nice clean room. Captain Johnson is so interested in his job, that after 25 years, he has been working steadily, and never missed a run.

Jeremy

Sonny Willard, Age 7, Second Grade, Klukwan School

I Like to See the Sun

I like to see the sun
and the eagles fly.
They float like a piece
of cotton. And the
waitresses give good
food and I like to
watch the T.V.

Nicole VanHorn
Age 6, First Grade
Holy Name School (Ketchikan)

Lots and Lots and Lots

My ferry boat, it has lots of people and lots of fun and lots of food and T.V. and lots of games and beds and soft pillows and cars and the deck and the captain.

Carlito Villanueva
Age 7, First Grade
Holy Name School (Ketchikan)

Casey Buser, Age 9, Third Grade, Unalaska School

The *Columbia*

Hello, my name is *Columbia.* I am the flagship of the Alaska Marine Highway System, a fleet of ferries in Alaska. I've been traveling the Alaska waters for many years. Hopefully, I will continue for many more years.

When people and cars come on board, I feel as if a great burden has been cast upon me. I warm up my engine and start to advance into the channel. Slowly I proceed out of Tongass Narrows (Ketchikan) feeling a great sense of relief as I venture out into the wide-open water. I observe fish, whales, seals, sea lions, porpoises, eagles and many other sea creatures.

Continuing along, I start to tire. The currents begin to push and toss me around. I strike logs often, and they dent and scar my sides.

As I approach the Juneau dock I give a great sigh of relief. I have the feeling of being as light as a feather, due to the unloading of the cars and people. In a couple of hours more cars and people start to board. Again I feel the burden start to build. As I warm up my engine and disembark from the dock at Juneau I feel free and joyful but then I remember the heavy burden of the cars and people and begin to be distressed.

When the people stroll about me, I feel a new sensation, a feeling of being tickled. I start to laugh. The engine sputters, then it returns to normal.

In the deep, dark night, it seems as if I am blind so I rely on the radar and spotlights to guide me. It is a very eerie feeling to go forward and not know exactly where you're going. Then as the sun breaks over the snowcapped mountains, the air feels crisp and cold and I feel safe again.

Suddenly I feel a terrible scrape on my belly. My engine stops promptly. Everybody on board is panicking. Water is leaking into my belly. I feel cold and scared. My Captain sends out an S.O.S.

Soon a large Coast Guard vessel comes to my rescue. The Coast Guard ship tows me back to Ketchikan, where all the passengers and cargo are unloaded. I am towed to the new drydock in Ketchikan. I sit there for what seems like forever. I long to ride on the water again and feel the cold, brisk waves rush by me.

As the workers repair me I feel stronger and healthier. Then the day arrives when I can sail the ocean and see all the beautiful sights and enjoy the cold air rushing by me.

I am back in the water now and I feel free and joyful. As the crowd cheers I sail off into the sunset for another voyage.

Scott McDonald
Eighth Grade
Thorne Bay

COLUMB

Ezra Sbonek, Age 7, Correspondence, Point Baker

Angela McCormick, Age 7, First Grade, Chiniak School

Being a ferry captain for so long, Captain Johnson has met all kinds of interesting and famous people. Some people that he has met include Linda Wagner, Herb Albert, Robert Norton Junior, lots of governors of different states, state officials, the Swedish Ambassador of Canada, and the Appointed Governor to the Yukon.

Jeremy

Kelly Winter
Age 11, Sixth Grade
Floyd Dryden Middle School (Juneau)

Bumblebee and Stacks

My brother and I had fun on the ferry playing transformers with a lot of other kids. I was always Bumblebee and Clint, my brother, was usually Stacks. Bumblebee is a little yellow volkswagon with a three on the hood. Some of us were deceptors and the rest were transformers. The transformers are good and deceptors are bad. I was a transformer so was my brother Clint. We pretended to fight until we got tired.

We also played a game called Treasure Hunt. We hunted for a map. A kid had a dad that worked on the ferry at least I think it was his dad. He would hide clues, then two kids would have to follow each clue until they found the map, then they would go back to the other kids and tell them that they found the map.

Shirley Doreen Wilson
Age 10, Third Grade
Nichen Cove School

Andrew Hotch, Age 11, Fourth Grade, Klukwan School

Carrie Valentine, Age 12, Sixth Grade, Floyd Dryden Middle School (Juneau)

Pat Blunt, Fourth Grade, Unalaska School

The second interview I had was with the Chief Engineer. He is responsible for all electronics, except for the Radio and the Radar. He is also responsible for all mechanical systems aboard the vessel, including water plants, and sewage treatment. Actually, the Chief Engineer manages all the other engineers, but doesn't get much hands-on work. He also does all of the paperwork, like payrolls, and keeps files for information on all the equipment, so they have a complete history of every mechanical item on the ferry. Using these histories, they can guess pretty accurately the time when the instrument will break down.

Jeremy

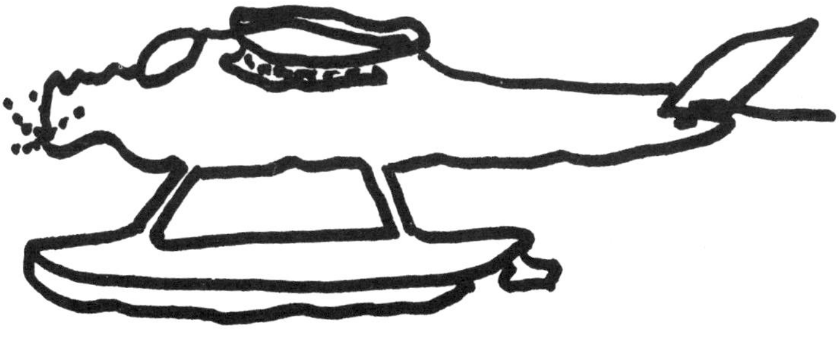

Stephen Dyer
Age 12, Sixth Grade
Floyd Dryden Middle School (Juneau)

Going Home to Rowan Bay

I went south for Christmas and we came back on the ferry boat, the *Malaspina.* We went through Queen Charlotte Sound and it was really bad and rough.

I like to sit in the lounge, because it was cool. I like to watch the waves move swiftly across the water. We got to take pictures of the snowy mountains and the different towns we went by. I liked it when we saw a porpoise beside the boat and it would jump like a fish and race the boat. When we went to eat dinner we saw an Indian man and he was selling necklaces and earrings that he made himself.

It took us four days to get to Petersburg from Seattle. From Petersburg we flew to Rowan Bay, Alaska where I live.

Meridith Simmons
Age 12, Sixth Grade
Rowan Bay School

GULP!

My long tongue extends out, slowly,
Slowly down go the cars.
Going, down, down, down. And GULP!
I close my mouth, move on.
At the next port, I burp some up.

Ken Brown
Age 13, Sixth Grade
Hoonah Elementary School

The Queen of the Sea

She skims through the ice-blue sea,
With waves crashing at her breast,
Surging, splitting snowy crest of wave,
While seagulls soar free.

Black clouds loom over,
Freeing lightning upon the ship,
Thunder roaring for all to hear,
Capturing the ferry in its horrid grip,
But the cries for help fall upon deaf ears.

Tossed back and forth like a ball,
Along comes a wave forty foot tall,
Overcomes the vessel but she stays afloat,
She would have capsized by now,
If it had been another boat.

Gathering her strength,
She uses all of her might,
Raises her head with pride,
Then powers through the storm
And into the night.

Her port ahead,
Of the storm she is free,
It's no wonder she's known as,
The Queen of the Sea.

Josh Meller
Age 13, Eighth Grade
George Gilson Junior High School (Valdez)

Stanley Ray Hotch, Age 11, Sixth Grade, Klukwan School

There are two paths you can take to become an engineer. One is that you can stand watch for three years of time (which can take over five years), and then take the test for the 3rd Assistant Engineer's License. After a year comes the 2nd Assistant Engineer's License, followed after another year by the 1st Engineer's License, and last comes the Chief Engineer's License. All of these licenses have two different types, a Motor Vessel License, or a Steam Vessel License.

The other path you can take to become an engineer is to go to school. Altogether there are six schools you can go to, five state schools, and one federal school, each of which takes four years. When you graduate, you have a Bachelor of Science and a license.

Jeremy

Janel Taylor
Age 12, Sixth Grade
Floyd Dryden Middle School (Juneau)

From Dutch Harbor to Seward

The Ferry takes you places.
You travel from Dutch Harbor to Seward.
You can see whales from the deck.
You can see fish from the windows.
You can hear the laughter from the people
and from the water.
They are excited.
Soon they will be seeing friends.

Maya Liepa
Age 9, Fourth Grade
Dutch Harbor

Kendra Yates
Age 11, Sixth Grade
Floyd Dryden Middle School (Juneau)

Ferry Lullaby

Little baby
go to sleep
let the waves rock you gently.
Close your eyes
little one
let the ferry be your bed.

Megan Travis
Age 7, Second Grade
Chiniak School

On the Way to Sitka

Once I went on a ferry to Sitka. It was cold and windy, and sometimes boring. It took seventeen hours to get there. We stopped at some places like Haines, but it was a long ways to town so we couldn't get any film until we got to Sitka.

Jamie L. Joey
Age 11
Marie Drake Middle School (Juneau)

Northern Lights

It was 12:00 a.m., and my family was on the ferry to go to Juneau. We brought sleeping bags but my mom and I read almost all night.

I tried to go to sleep but the floor was hard and I had a backache and my brother Jeff was snoring and there was a baby crying.

The waves were crashing against the front windows but it was a very clear night. Finally I fell asleep and I was dreaming of me on a big board flying in space. Right when I was falling off, my dad woke me up and said, "Kay, come on outside."

When I got outside, he said "Look at the sky." I looked and saw the Northern Lights. They were all different colors and they were changing shape. I felt dizzy looking up for so long.

My dad said it was late and that I should go back to sleep.

I snuggled back in my sleeping bag and fell asleep right away.

Honk. Honk. I woke up to the low, loud honk of the ferry. We were in Juneau.

It was early in the morning and people were crowding off the ferry. We got on the car deck and into our truck. We waited a long time to get off.

Finally it was our turn. We went up the steep ramp and then we were on our way to the hotel.

Kay von Rekowski
Age 10, Fourth Grade
Hoonah Elementary School

The Aurora shimmers across the sky like curtains of rainbow.

Alexis Delbridge, Age 10, Weller School (Fairbanks)

Terry Palagyi, Age 8, Third Grade, McNeil Canyon School (Homer)

The Chief Engineer has had some unforgettable experiences aboard the ferry, a couple of which he told to me. One story about a steward went like this: one day a drunk was put onto the ferry, and he went straight to the bar. He stayed there, consuming more and more alcohol until 2:00 a.m., when the bar had to close. When the barkeeper finally got him out of the bar, the drunk headed for the restrooms. When he got there, a steward was cleaning them out, and told the drunk to go around the corner to the other bathroom. He then continued cleaning. The steward suddenly felt something wasn't right, and spun around just in time to catch a knife that the drunk was trying to stab him with.

Some other things that are unforgettable are when the crankcase blows out. Fire shoots out with a loud roar, and black smoke covers everything. Also, the ferry has a bunch of black pipes that carry hot oil, and when those burst and the oil hits something else hot, it ignites and makes an awful mess. Another explosion that occured was when a 3KW generator was started. The yolk fell down into the rack causing it to jam open, causing gas to pour out, which eventually exploded.

Jeremy

(Editor's Note: Although these problems can occur, Alaska Marine Highway has a strong safety record due to the foresight and competence of highly trained personnel like the Chief Engineer and the Captain.)

You Mite See

You mite see some sea lions on a bell buoy. You mite see a lot of seals on an ilend. Maybe a whale jumping out of the watter. Or another boat on the water. If your lucky you mite be the only one that sees a watterfal very beauteful.

Jacob Tennessen
Age 6, First Grade
Chiniak School

Jacob Tennessen, Age 6, First Grade, Chiniak School

THE CIRCUS FERRY

It was a joy on the circus ferry,
Lots of clowns,
        pigeons,
                and a canary,
Lots of popcorn,
        hot dogs,
                pizza, and
                        pop,
Souvenirs of all kinds,
        plus it was hot.

The skinny man jumped into the water.
The fat lady jumped in too.
And LAST they threw in you know who!
                        SPLASH!!

Josh Delbridge
Age 9
Weller Elementary (Fairbanks)

Ride on the *Columbia*

When I rode on the *Columbia* ferry, I thought it was cool. We rode from Ketchikan to Seattle. When we went past the *Walla Walla* (Washington State Ferry) it was really rough. My sister and I stood in the middle of the cabin and when the boat went one way we went back and forth.

Tracey R. Huret
Age 10, Fourth Grade
Rowan Bay School

Biology Class on the *Malaspina*

When Sitka High biology teacher, Mr. Bill Foster, learned that six students would be gone for four days on a swimming team trip to Ketchikan, he decided to send along a unit on earthworm ecology, the same subject students in class would be covering.

Foster prepared a small suitcase containing all materials needed - living and preserved earthworms, dissecting sets, reference material and other items to complete the exercise.

Early in the trip the six students, John Goodness, Cheryl Gilmour, Bruce Hays, Ida Williams, Mary Ann Goodman, and Greg Mears gathered in the *Malaspina* cafeteria to begin. It was reported to have attracted quite a crowd of onlookers.

When the students returned four days later they did not have to make up class work. They also found an interesting diversion on the long trip to Ketchikan. Foster commented, "Of historic note, it was probably the first earthworm dissection on an Alaska Marine Highway Ferry." Also, he stated he would like to develop other traveling units related to water quality and natural history that could be carried by student ferry travelers.

From *Pushka Press*,
Sitka High School newspaper
November 24, 1976

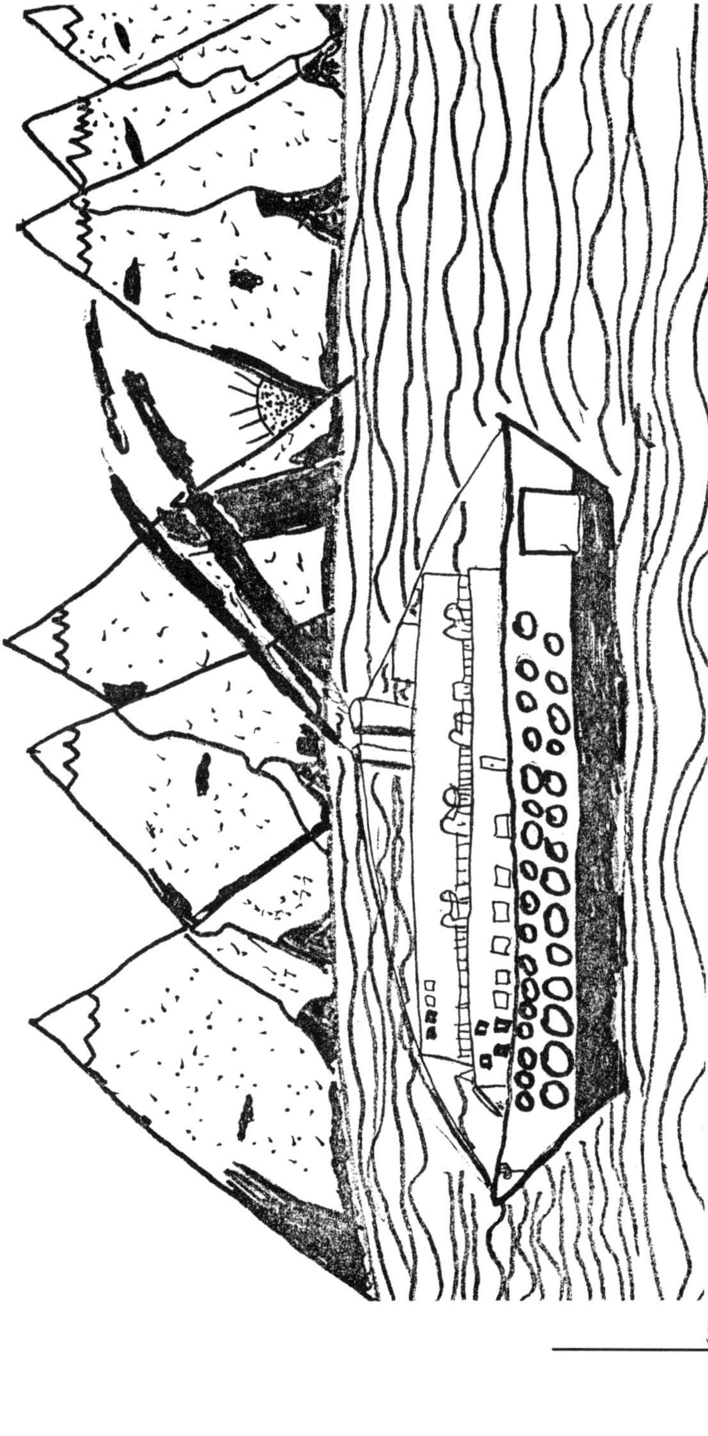

Elsa Endorf, Age 12, Sixth Grade, Floyd Dryden Middle School (Juneau)

Our Adventure Trip on a Ferry

On the ferry we had lots of fun,
We ate candy and chewed lots of gum.

We watched porpoises, jellyfish, eagles,
and whales,
We watched and watched and were
splashed by their tails.

On the car deck we saw cats, poodles,
and a ferret,
We visited him and fed him a carrot.

Our cabin was number three,
Who was on the top bunk? — Just me!

As we played Spy Hunter on the
video games,
My brother kept calling me names.

We played cards, tag, see-saw, and
chess,
Then went to the sundeck for
a rest.

All day we heard the pounding of waves,
At night we watched the red and green maze.

Class Composite poem, Third Grade
Ms. Mabel Murray, Teacher
Holy Name School (Ketchikan)

The Ferry can be Very Nice

The Ferry can be very nice.
The water splashing on the side.
You sleep and eat and walk and talk.
And do almost anything you ought.
You watch the seagulls far above.
And watch a movie just for fun.
And if you want, you can make a friend,
And you can play together on the way back again!

Tania Abello
Age 9, Third Grade
Unalaska

Blind Man and His Seeing Eye Dog

Our group got split up on different floors. While some of us were trying to find the other group we just about knocked this blind man down. The guy had a seeing eye dog with him. The dog was really pretty. It was as black as tar. The blind man needed help finding the observation lounge so I helped him. In the beginning I didn't know quite what to do but then he told me to just walk in front of the dog and the dog would follow me. I led him into the observation lounge and he thanked me.

Johanna Painter
Age 11, Sixth Grade
Marie Drake Middle School (Juneau)

Troy Bundy, Age 9, Third Grade, Unalaska School

When the Chief Engineer was asked if he could start over, "Would you choose the same career", he also answered with a definite sounding, "Absolutely!" He had been raised on the water, and when he was 17 he was fortunate enough to get started on his career. If it were possible, he says he would never retire. It was the perfect career for him to choose. A good aspect of his job is that the work schedule allows for a good family life.

His contract also provides many benefits, such as health insurance and retirement paychecks. It is interesting work, always changing and giving opportunity for learning new things.

Jeremy

Bonnie Merculief, Age 13, Sixth Grade, Angoon

Eagle

The *Aurora* rumbled under my tired feet. I breathed a sigh of relief as the majestic peaks rose before me.

Above me, in the shining blue sky, soared an eagle so gracefully that it appeared to be attached to unseen strings. It dipped its mighty wings and circled the boat, I watched enthralled at the beauty of the great bird who symbolizes freedom for everyone in this country.

Mary Brady
Ninth Grade
Thorne Bay School

Christine Lau, Age 8, Second Grade, Chiniak School

Meghan Mutch, Third Grade, Unalaska School

Whale Watchers Certificate

I like the ferries. It is very fun on them. I came from Seattle on the *Columbia*. It is very big. I like to walk around the ferry. It is fun to explore. Once I got a whale watchers certificate. I am very glad they have ferries in Alaska. I went to Kake on the *LeConte*. It was beautiful.

Paul Sarter
Age 11
Klukwan School

Noah Hanson
Age 6, Correspondence
Wrangell

The Scenery at Night

Sometimes late at night
When I look off the docks at the star light,
I look at all the sea animals
And what a beautiful sight!
I want to jump in the water with them
And I just might!

Brandy Ketchum
Age 11, Sixth Grade
Chiniak School

Cash Stanford, Age 10, Klukwan School

John Kenneth George
Age 12, Sixth Grade
Floyd Dryden Middle School (Juneau)

What I Do and Don't Like To Do on the Ferry

I like riding the ferry.

I like the place where you eat, because the ice cream and sweet foods look so good! Almost every time I ride the ferry I have a frozen ice cream bar. It hurts my teeth because it is so cold! I like the cakes and the orange juice too!

I don't like the car deck because it is too noisy. It hurts my ears. I don't like the elevators because they make me dizzy.

I like our stateroom because I like the bunk-beds. At first I don't like to climb the ladders but after I do it a few times I like it

Amy Weishahn
Age 7, Second Grade
Correspondence (Haines)

Humungous, Enormous

I saw a whale ten feet from the boat. It leaped about like five feet out of the water. The whale went head first into the water. Its tail made a humungous, enormous splash.

Caleb Walser
Age 7, Second Grade
Chiniak School

Wait Till After

All of our family get to go.
We were waiting in the ferry.
Kenneth took our popcorn away.
He wouldn't share it.
He said wait till after.
I bet he ate it up.
Some men were laying down sleeping.
We went on the ferry lots of times I think.
The end.

Rudy Willard
Age 5, Kindergarten
Klukwan School

Tom Crandall
Age 8, Third Grade
Unalaska School

Erik Reimnitz, Age 12, Seventh Grade, McMurray Middle School, (Vashon Island, Washington)

The editors wish to express their appreciation to the following teachers who encouraged their students to submit entries to the Alaskan Ferry Tale contest held in the spring of 1987.

Wilma Adams, Unalaska Elementary School, Dutch Harbor
Jean Ann Alter, Centralized Correspondence, Juneau
Jaxine Anderson, Corrrespondence, Haines
Bob Andrews, Klukwan School
Margaret Andrews, Klukwan School
Don Bailey, Nikolaevsk School, Anchor Point
Jetta Budd, Hoonah Public Schools
A. J. Dilworth, Dolomi
George Eckey, Angoon High School
Melanie Engram, Unalaska Elementary School, Dutch Harbor
Bob Falle, Correspondence, Point Baker
William L. Foster, Sitka High School
Larry Garrison, George H. Gilson Junior High,Valdez
Lela Grogan, Correspondence, Juneau
Barbara Guenther, Rowan Bay School
Angelika Hall, Wrangell
Alice Hanson, Correspondence, Wrangell
Alan Hauan, Revilla High School, Ketchikan
Teresa Hura, Klukwan School
Susan Johnson, Holy Name School, Ketchikan
Lynn Jorgensen, Holy Name School, Ketchikan
Barbara Knoll, Correspondence, Douglas
Lesley Lyman, Marie Drake Middle School, Juneau
Liz Marantz, Klukwan School
Claudia McConnell, Hoonah Public Schools

Betty McKey, Klukwan School
Ms. Mabel Murray, Holy Name School, Ketchikan
Sally Navarre, Correspondence, Seal Bay
Ron Nelson, Tracyton Elementary, Silverdale (Washington)
Michael J. O'Connell, Mt. Bether Bible Center, Hoonah
Mary Lou Pervis, Correspondence, Douglas
Rita Pfenninger, McNeil Canyon Elementary, Homer
Deborah C. Piper, McNeil Canyon Elementary, Homer
Shari Roths, Nichen Cove School
Nicki Shelton, Hoonah
Mary Ann Soltys, Floyd Dryden Middle School, Juneau
Donald Spink, Thorne Bay School
Arnold Strong, Tenakee Springs School
Karen Tennessen, Chiniak School
Pam Wilson, Correspondence, Wrangell
Mrs. Wooten, Whittier School
Tim Young, Hydaburg

CONTRIBUTORS' NOTES as of March 15, 1987 (unless otherwise noted)

Editors Mosley, Delbridge, and Evans held a contest in March, 1987, for students in schools ranging from Southeastern Alaska to the Aleutians asking for stories, poems, and artwork. Over forty schools entered. The focus was on travel and life aboard Alaska's nine ferries. Prizes were awarded in three areas including artwork, story, and poetry in two separate categories: Kindergarten through fourth grades and fifth through high school.

FOURTH GRADE CLASS from Hoonah Elementary School. "This is a poem our class wrote about animals you can see from the ferry. There are fifteen students in our class. Their names are: Richard, Angie, Sharon, Laura, Linette, Howard, Gerald, Leroy, Kay, Jason, Tina, Jennifer, Leetta, Lycen, and Dessy. We live on an island and the ferry or an airplane are the only ways we can travel to Juneau or anywhere." Claudia McConnell is their teacher.

THE CLASS OF '93 is the sixth grade class from Hoonah. They have been reading, writing and listening to poetry for two months. They like writing poems and riding the ferry. Students include: Russ Dalton, Jennifer Shandy, Ken Brown, Brindle Budd, Kamal Lindoff, Roy Hill, Robert Sharclane, Gus Mills, Corinna Quilliam, and Gretchen Oliver. Their teacher is Jetta Budd.

THIRD GRADE CLASS from Holy Name School in Ketchikan. "We put all of our experiences together and came up with this poem." Their teacher is Ms. Mabel A. Murray.

TANIA ABELLO is from Unalaska and in the third grade.

JEREMIAH (JEREMY) K. ANDREWS was12 years old and in the 7th grade at Klukwan School when he completed his anecdote. He won second place for "Ol' Brake Light." His anecdote appeared in *Northwest Ferry Tales*. Jeremy did the interviews a year later when he was 13 years old. His hobbies include "girls, computers, reading, writing, and coin collecting."

GEORGI BASARGIN is in the fifth grade, and attends Nikolaevsk Elementary School in Anchor Point. He won second place in art division. His drawing is not included in the book because of difficulties in reproducing it.

JOSH P. BATCHELOR from Juneau. "I am 12 years old. I've lived in Alaska for three years now. I attend Dryden Middle School and I'm in the sixth grade. I live with my mom and dad and a brother and sister. I have not ridden on the ferry yet but this summer I might with my mom. I'm looking forward to it." He received an honorable mention in art.

MICHAEL BITTNER is from Dutch Harbor and attends Unalaska School. He is in the fourth grade.

PAT BLUNT is from Unalaska School and is in the fourth grade.

TIM BOTZ is six years old and in the first grade at Chiniak School on Kodiak Island. He states that he likes dinosaurs.

MARY BRADY is from Thorne Bay and in the ninth grade. She states "I've lived in Alaska for 11 years and loved every minute of it. I like to write, draw, and play basketball. I live out of Thorne Bay about a mile and a half and the only way to get to my house is by boat. I am interested in journalism and art."

KENNETH (KEN) S. BROWN, a sixth grader, states, "I was born October 8, 1974, in Juneau, Alaska. At the age of three I moved to Hoonah. Between that time and now I've had many fun, interesting and relaxing rides on the ferry." He was a second place winner in contest. His poem appeared in *Northwest Ferry Tales.*

TROY BUNDY is from Unalaska School and lives in Dutch Harbor. He is nine years old and in the third grade.

CASEY BUSER is nine years old and in the third grade. He attends Unalaska School.

TOM CRANDALL is 8 years old and in the third grade at Unalaska School.

AMY DARLING, attended Tracyton Elementary in Silverdale, Washington, at the time of submitting her contribution in 1988. She says "I am nine years old. My birthday is April 24, 1978. I have two sisters and four brothers. I was born in Washington. I now live in Homer, Alaska. Alaska is my favorite place. I like the people and schools in Homer." Amy's poem was submitted in 1988.

BETHANY JOY DAVIDSON, a seven year old says, "I was born in Cordova but lived in Klukwan most of my life. I live with my mom and brother. We don't have any pets."

ALEXIS DELBRIDGE submitted her drawing of the Northern Lights at age 10 in 1989. She attends Rosamond Weller School in Fairbanks with her brother Josh. She is editor Delbridge's granddaughter.

JOSH DELBRIDGE attends Rosamond Weller Elementary School in Fairbanks. Josh's poem was submitted in 1988 when he was nine. He is the grandson of editor Joyce Delbridge.

MICHELLE DILBECK is eleven years old, has lived in Juneau for five years and in Anchorage for one year before that. She attends Dryden Middle School in Juneau and is in the sixth grade. She stays that she "rode on a ferry one time to Hoonah just for fun."

STEPHEN DYER is twelve years old, attends Dryden Middle School in Juneau and says that he has a good personality and keeps good average grades. He has traveled on the Alaskan Ferry System to Sitka during last summer vacation.

ERIN EDDY is in the second grade at Holy Name School in Ketchikan. She says, "I love to take ferry rides to places." She tied for second place in her division.

ELSA ENDORF is twelve years old and attends Dryden Middle School in Juneau. She has one sister and one brother, and has lived in Juneau for five years. She states "I have ridden the ferry system twenty one times. I like it very much. I like hiking and playing in the snow. I help collect toys in the 4-H toy drive. Living in Alaska is fun."

DANIEL GASTON "lice to bro and bo art werc (likes to draw and do art work)." He is 7 years old and lives in Juneau. He is on correspondence studies. His picture was chosen for the cover illustration, and received an honorable mention in art in the contest.

JOHN KENNETH GEORGE is twelve years old and attends Dryden Middle School in Juneau. He is in the sixth grade and has lived in Juneau for 12 years. He states "I've been to Sitka and Petersburg on swim meets. We went on a ferry."

ERIK GROVE, age 10, is a fourth grade student at Rowan Bay School. Erik tells us "I am about four feet tall. I like sports and writing sories. I like hunting and fishing."

BECKY MARIE HALE is 11 year old and in the fifth grade at Rowan Bay School. She says that she lives seven miles from Rowan Bay "and it is fun."

NOAH HANSON, a six year old, lives in Wrangell and is on correspondence studies. Noah states "I am a little boy. I live on Zimovia Strait close to Thoms Place. My pop has a fishing boat named *Sea Crest* and I go trolling with him in the summer. In the winter I play in the snow and run around our new house." He received an honorable mention in art division.

LUCAS HARRINGTON is in the second grade at Holy Name School in Ketchikan. He tied for second place in his division.

HEATHER HIEBERT from Dolomi is 13 years old and lives in a floating logging camp. She received an honorable mention in art.

AARON HOTCH is seven years old and in the second grade. He lives in Klukwan.

ANDREW HOTCH lives in Klukwan. He is eleven years old and in the fourth grade.

DONALD S. HOTCH, JR. says "I love computer games, sports, and riding the three-wheeler." He goes to Klukwan Elementary School, is twelve years old and in the seventh grade.

ELLA HOTCH is in the first grade, is seven years old and attends Klukwan School.

STANLEY RAY HOTCH is eleven and in the sixth grade at Klukwan School.

KANE HUFF is seven years old and in the first grade. He attends Rowan Bay School, and says "I live in a logging camp on an island by Sitka. If we want to go anywhere we have to fly."

TRACEY R. HURET is ten years old and in the fourth grade at Rowan Bay School.

JAMIE L. JOEY is in the sixth grade at Marie Drake Middle School in Juneau, is eleven years old, and likes reading and math.

ANISIM KALUGIN is 12 years old, from Anchor Point and attends Nikolaevsk School, states, "I speak two languages - Russian and English - and I go to sixth grade. I have dark blond hair and my sports are basketball and volleyball and I had a dislocated arm."

LUBA KALUGIN is 12 and in the sixth grade at Nikolaevsk School. She states "I like sports. My hair is black. I wear eyeglasses. I like to read books. I am a Russian girl. I like to go to school. My best sport is basketball, my eyes are brown, I like to exercise, my best subject is reading and spelling. I like snow."

BRANDY KETCHUM is in the sixth grade, and says "I live in Chiniak with my mom, dad, and brother Ricky." She is 11 years old.

DEANNA L. KING goes to Klukwan School, is 13 years old and in the eighth grade. She says "I am a very active person. I like to read. I was born in December. I live in Klukwan. I've lived here all my life. I was born in Wrangell. I have three step brothers and one step sister. I am about 5 foot 5 inches."

LISA LARSON likes "to do experiments, like making different sounds and colors." She is six years old in the first grade at Rowan Bay School and adds that she likes to play with the new kids in the summer.

CHRISTINE LAU is from Chiniak School, in the second grade and is eight years old. She says she has "a litle sister and a big sister," and adds "my dog just had puppies." She likes living in Alaska, and came from Florida.

JACOB de LEON, a student at Unalaska School in the Aleutians, is ten years old and in the third grade.

MAYA LIEPA is nine years old and in the fourth grade. She lives in Dutch Harbor. She is a first place winner in story division.

DAVID B. LILLY is five years old, is in kindergarten and attends Taku Elementary School in Anchorage.

DANIELLE LUDWIGSEN is a first grader at Holy Name School in Ketchikan.

ANGELA McCORMICK lives near the ocean in a red house, is seven years old and in the first grade at Chiniak School. She says "I have a big white dog." She likes to read.

SCOTT McDONALD lives in Thorne Bay, and is in the eighth grade. He is a first place winner in writing.

JOSH M. MELLER, age 13 and in the eighth grade at George Gilson Junior High School in Valdez, states he was "born in Alaska and have lived here all my life. I enjoy sports, motorcycles, and rock music. I get good grades and have three varsity letters in basketball and wrestling." He is a first place winner in poetry division.

BONNIE MERCULIEF, age 13 and in the sixth grade, states "I live in Angoon. I love to draw and read poetry. I stay with my grandparents." She received an honorable mention in art.

MEGHAN MUTCH is in the third grade at Unalaska School on the Aleutian Chain.

JOHANNA PAINTER, age 11, says "I like to swim and roller skate. I am on a soccer team." She attends Marie Drake Middle School in Juneau.

ROBBY PALAGYI , 7 years old and in the second grade at McNeil Canyon School. He says "I live in Homer, Alaska. I have blond hair and brown eyes. My birthday is August 18, 1979. I have a brother TJ and a sister Annie. My hobby is all sports. We have fifteen animals. I like candy. I like to draw and clean. I like ferries."

TERRY PALAGYI, is 8 years old and will be nine in two weeks, says "I have blond hair, and blue eyes. I have a basset hound named Gus. My hobbies are drawing vehicles, swimming, and reading." He is a second place winner in art division. He is from Homer and attends McNeil Canyon School. He is a third grader.

ROBERT PARSONS. "I am twelve years old. I attend Dryden Middle School in Juneau, Alaska, and I'm in the sixth grade. I have lived in Alaska for twelve years. I live with my dad Jamie, mom Mary Beth, brother Andrew, sister Sara and my cat Tiger. We have traveled the Alaskan ferry system to Skagway because my father wanted to go with his team for a softball tournament."

PUSHKA PRESS, Sitka High School newspaper (November 24, 1976). No author is listed for article.

LUKE RANDALL is on correspondence studies. He is six years old, in the first grade and states "I live in Seal Bay on Afognak Island and I am almost seven. There are lots of magpies around my house and brown bears and sea otters. We have some pet deer. My family runs a hunting and fishing lodge. We have no neighbors. We have a tame seagull too."

ERIK REIMNITZ is 12 years old and in the seventh grade at McMurray Middle School on Vashon Island in Washington. He states, "I was born on April 27, 1976 in Kodiak, Alaska. Now I live on Vashon Island and go every summer up to Kodiak. I like to go with my father and his salmon-fishing boat. My hobbies are drawing, playing piano and all types of sports." He likes to draw the animals he sees on his father's boat. Erik's drawings were submitted early 1989. Four were chosen for the book.

KAY VON REKOWSKI. "I live in Hoonah, Alaska. I like to play outside in the woods. I iceskate and skateboard. My favorite color is blue. I like to write stories and I play violin." Kay is ten years old and in the fourth grade. She is a first place winner in writing.

AMY RICHARDSON lives in Hoonah and says she likes to write stories and poems. She is 13 and in the seventh grade. She won an Honorable Mention for her poem.

KATIE ANN ROONEY is in the third grade at Unalaska School in Dutch Harbor.

PAUL SARTER, age 11, is from Klukwan School.

EZRA SBONEK is on Correspondence Studies and from Point Baker. He is seven years old. He says "I like to ride the ferry and I like to fly, too." He is a first place winner.

MERIDITH SIMMONS is 12 years old and attends Rowan Bay School. Her story won an honorable mention in the contest.

CASH STANFORD is ten years old and goes to Klukwan School.

JAIME STANFORD is in kindergarten at Klukwan School. She won an Honorable Mention in writing.

J. P. STELZER is eight years old, and in the third grade, and says "I live in Chiniak. We built our house. I like to sing, play on the computer and play outside."

JEREMY STONE says "I live in the community of Chiniak on Kodiak Island in Alaska. I am 10 years old and in third grade. I go to Chiniak School. I like to fish, camp out, travel, and have adventures. I like math and science and to write in cursive."

DANNY MATHEW SUBRAMANIAN is twelve, in the sixth grade and attends Klukwan Elementary School.

JANEL TAYLOR is a twelve year old girl who attends Dryden Middle School in Juneau. She is in the sixth grade, and states that she went with her Girl Scout troop to Haines, Wrangell and Sitka. She has also gone to Skagway and Ketchikan with her family.

JACOB TENNESSEN is six years old and attends Chiniak School. He says "I like to read. My favorite books are about animals and science. My little brother is Travis."

COLETTE THOMPSON is a first grade student attending Holy Name School in Ketchikan.

MEGAN TRAVIS, age 7, attends Chiniak School. She says "I have blonde hair and blue eyes. My favorite food is crab. I like to draw and read and walk in the waves on the beach."

CARRIE VALENTINE is twelve and attends Dryden Middle School. She is in the sixth grade. She has lived in Juneau for seven years and travels the Alaska ferries every summer, and sometimes to Skagway to visit relatives.

NICOLE VANHORN, age 6 and in the first grade, attends Holy Name School in Ketchikan.

CARLITO VILLANUEVA is in the first grade at Holy Name School in Ketchikan.

TRACY WALLACE is twelve, in the sixth grade at Dryden Middle School in Juneau, and lives with her mom, dad, sister, brother, and four dogs. She tells us that her class has traveled on the ferry to Petersburg to visit the Little Norway Festival.

CALEB WALSER attends Chiniak School. He is seven years old and in the second grade. He comments "I do good in spelling, math, and reading. I feel good about myself."

AMY WEISHAHN lives on the Haines Highway. She says, "I'm seven years old and I'm on correspondence. I have a baby doll named Crystal."

RUDY WILLARD , age 5, attends Klukwan School and is in kindergarten.

SONNY WILLARD is seven years old, in the second grade and attends Klukwan School

SHIRLEY WILSON, age 10 years, says "I live on a log camp. My uncle owns the log camp." She is in the third grade and attends Nichen Cove School.

KELLY WINTER is 11 years old in the sixth grade, and attends Dryden Middle School in Juneau, and states "I have lived in Alaska for nine years. I live with my mom Chris, my dad Bob, my brother Craig, and my two dogs Splash and Gabe." Kelly received an honorable mention in art.

KENDRA YATES is eleven years old, attends Dryden Middle School in Juneau, and is in the sixth grade. Kendra states "I have lived in Alaska for 1-1/2 years with my parents. I have traveled the Alaska Ferry

System to Canada for vacation."

HAI HAN YE goes to Whittier School. He is 13 years old and states, "I like to draw. My favorite things to draw are boats." He received a first place in art.

Robert Parsons
Age 12, Sixth Grade
Floyd Dryden Middle School (Juneau)

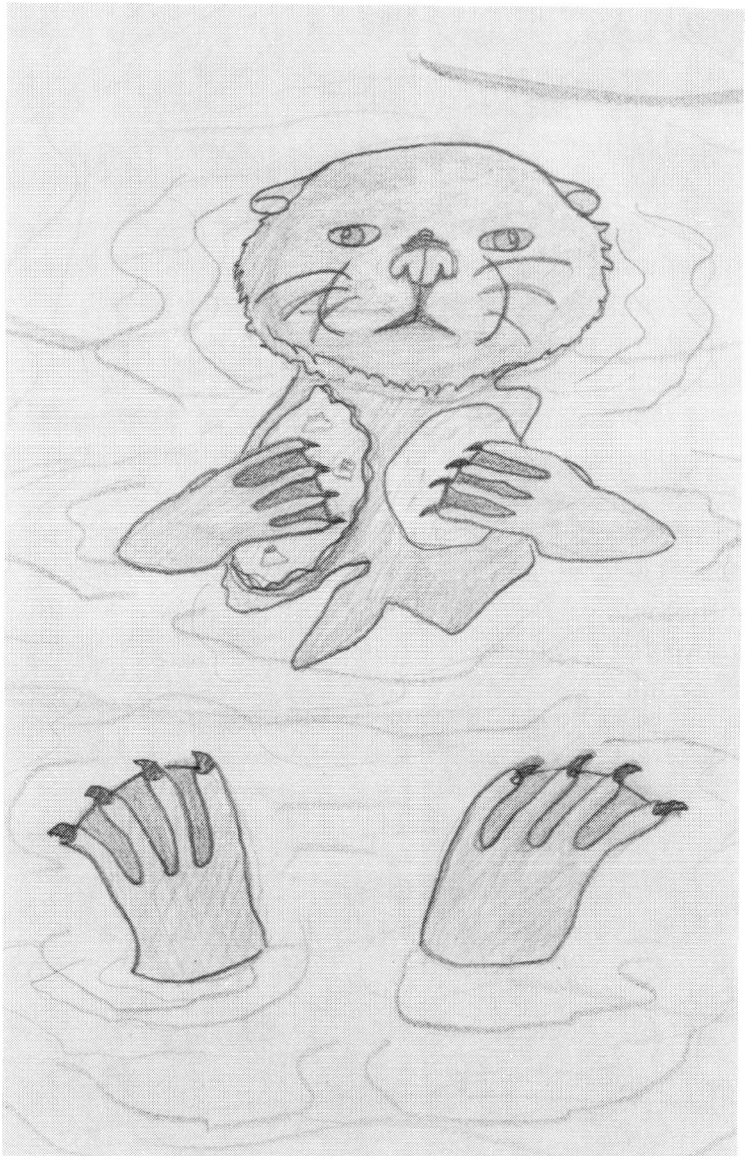

Erik Reimnitz
Age 12, Seventh Grade
McMurray Middle School, (Vashon Island, Washington)

EDITORS

Marilyn Cochran Mosley, Ed.D., a school psychologist, travels and works extensively throughout Alaska's schools and has personal contact with many teachers and students. She is the author/publisher of three children's books about dachshund travels in Alaska and Canada: *Dachshund Tails North, Dachshund Tails Up The Inside Passage,* and *Dachshund Tails Down The Yukon.*

Joyce Delbridge, retired teacher and writer, is editor/publisher of *Ferry Tales from Puget Sound,* an anthology of stories, poems, and artwork. This book sold 6,000 copies from April 1986, to December 30, 1988. Her second book *Northwest Ferry Tales,* also an anthology, was released in January 1989. She has also completed three juvenile books, and teaches a writing workshop.

Patricia Evans, a former teacher, is a free lance writer. She has completed a novel for girls and has had work published in various publications.

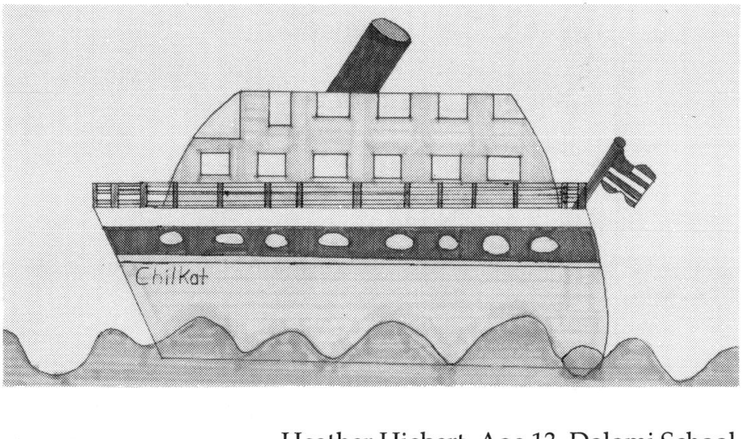

Heather Hiebert, Age 13, Dolomi School

FERRY FACTS AND HISTORY

The year 1949 marked the beginning of the ferry service in Alaska. A private operator ran the area's first ferry, a war surplus Navy landing craft, the *Chilkoot,* from Juneau to the upper Lynn Canal communities of Haines and Skagway. In 1957, the territorial government bought the *Chilkat* to replace the *Chilkoot.* Two years later Alaska became a state (1959).

The voters of the new state passed an18 million dollar bond issue in 1960, to build terminals and order four vessels. Between 1959 and 1962, the 99-foot *Chilkat* served from Haines to Juneau. Three sister ships, *Malaspina, Matanuska,* and *Taku,* began operating in the first six months of 1963. Each vessel measured 352 feet, and all operated on the Prince Rupert to Skagway route.

Alaska took delivery of the*Tustumena* in July of 1964, and initiated service to Kodiak. The system transported over 83,000 passengers and 16,000 vehicles that year. At that time the *Chilkat* moved to Prince William Sound, inaugurating service to Cordova from Valdez.

The Alaskan Marine Highway, the name given the ferry system, extended its route south to Seattle in December, 1967.

With the purchase of the *Wickersham* in April, 1968, and the *Bartlett,* the state brought its ferry fleet to seven. *Bartlett* was used in Prince William Sound. The *Chilkat* moved south and ran between Juneau and Hoonah.

In 1972 the *Malaspina* went into dry dock to be stretched 56 feet, from its original 352 feet to a new total length of 408 feet.

The *LeConte* joined the Alaska Marine Highway fleet in 1974, providing transportation to Hoonah and Kake. The *Chilkat* transferred once more, this time to the Ketchikan area, and provide service from Ketchikan to Hollis and Metlakatla. The system sold the *Wickersham* and took delivery of the *Columbia* in June of that year.

The newest of the fleet of nine vessels, the *Aurora* , was delivered and took over the routes in Southeast Alaska in 1977.

The system ordered another stretching in 1978, this time the *Matanuska* . It, too, became 408 feet in length and was used on the Southeast route. In July of 1985 service began to Stewart/Hyder during the summer months.

In 1988, Alaska Marine Highway officials selected Bellingham, Washington, to replace Seattle as the system's southern terminus. At publication date, however, ferries are still coming into Seattle's Pier 48. The change is scheduled for October 1989. The year 1988 also marked the Alaska Marine Highway's 25th anniversary.

The current system consists of nine vessels, travels 3,500 miles, and has three major routes. The Southeast Alaska Route cruises the glacier-carved fjords and forested islands of the Inside Passage, with views of the prime habitat for bald eagles, porpoises, sea lions and whales. Southeast Alaska is the home of Haida, Tlingit and Tsimshian Indians. Their rich heritage is reflected through their arts and crafts, which are displayed throughout the communities. The towns of Ketchikan, Wrangell, Petersburg, Sitka, Juneau, Haines and Skagway are on this route. The communities of Craig, Klawock, Metlakatla, Kake, Angoon, Tenakee, Hoonah, and Pelican are served by the Southeast Route.

The second major route is the Southcentral Route. More than half of Alaska's residents live in the popular coastal communities of Southcentral Alaska. While cruising along the gentle curve of the Gulf of Alaska, one can view spectacular ice blue glaciers, tranquil fjords, popular clamming beaches and salmon streams. Cordova, Valdez, Whittier, Seward, Homer, Seldovia, Kodiak, and Port Lions are included.

The third major route is the Southwest Alaska Route. Here the panorama ranges from the gentle grassland of the Aleutian Islands to the surreal volcanic landscape of Katmai National Park. It's the natural habitat for brown bear, sea otters, fur seals and seabirds, and a paradise for nature viewing. Ships of the Alaska Marine Highway make six scheduled stops between May and September to five southwest Alaskan communities which includes Chignik,

Sand Point, King Cove, Cold Bay, and Dutch Harbor.

More than 378,600 passengers and 99,500 vehicles ride the ferries each year. The ferries stop at 31 communities including Prince Rupert and Seattle. Ferries run according to tides and politics. What town gets which vessel is a constant battle at the Marine Highway headquarters and in the Alaska Legislature (which controls the budget).

The ferries sail around the clock. They keep many towns in milk, meat, fresh lettuce and fruit. They carry motorists, bikers and backpackers; villagers to their doctors; school athletes to their rivals' gym floors; winter-bound residents on weekend joyrides. Babies are born on board and there are, of course, shipboard deaths. Although some crew members on each sailing have received Emergency Medical Training, no professional medical service is available. During summer, passengers may enjoy the informative Naturalist programs presented by the U.S. Forest Service.

The four larger sister ships, the "mainliners," make the longest runs from Alaska to Seattle, Washington, and to Prince Rupert, British Columbia. They are one of Alaska's biggest tourist attractions, and provide a money-saving alternative to the cruise ships that share their waterways. The longest trip is between Seattle and Skagway, via Sitka, takes three and a half days and is approximately 1,150 nautical miles.

There is yet another route which surpasses the Southeast Alaska course in mileage and time underway. The *Tustumena* sails from Seward to Seattle once a year (sometime during the first week in January) for annual maintenance. The running time is approximately five days for the 1,500 nautical mile journey.

The one-hour run between Haines and Skagway is the shortest run. Dogs, cats, and other household pets are charged a fare of $10 to or from Seattle, and $5 to or from Prince Rupert.

The State of Alaska faces long-range questions about the future of its aging fleet. Some want to replace the "slow-but-steady" diesel vessels with speedier catamarans. Others say the fleet should be trimmed, that the State cannot keep a $63 million (yearly) ferry system afloat.

Luba Kalugin
Age 12, Sixth Grade
Nikolaevsk School (Anchor Point)

Erik Reimnitz, Age 12, Seventh Grade, McMurray Middle School, (Vashon Island, Washington)

THE FLEET

Aurora built by Peterson Shipbuilders in Sturgeon Bay, Wisconsin, andbegan service in 1977. **Length** is 235 feet long and **beam** is 57 feet. Its **draft** is 12 feet 9 inches; **horsepower** is 4,300. It can transport 250 passengers and 47 standard vehicles. **Service speed** is 14 knots. Food service, a cocktail lounge, and a solarium are provided. Crew required on board is 24.

Bartlett launched in 1968 at Jeffersonville, Indiana, and went into service from her home port of Cordova the following year. **Length** is 193 feet and **beam** is 53 feet. **Draft** is 13 feet; **horsepower** is 3,468. **Service speed** is 14 knots. It has a capacity for 38 standard vehicles, and a passenger capacity of 170. Food service and a solarium are provided. Crew required on board is 24.

Chilkat is the original ship of the Alaska Marine Highway fleet and was taken over by the State of Alaska following admission to the Union in 1959. Built in 1957 she serves the southern area between Ketchikan, Metlakatla, and Hollis. **Length** is slightly less than 100 feet, **beam** is 35 feet, **draft** is 8 feet, and **horsepower** is 730. She **cruises** at 10 knots. There is room aboard for 15 vehicles and 82 passengers. A crew of 7 is required on board.

Columbia is the largest ferry and is the flagship of the Marine Highway fleet. She was launched by Lockheed Shipbuilding in Seattle in 1973. **Length** is 418 feet, **beam** is 85 feet, **draft** is 17 feet, and **horsepower** is 12,350 with capacity for 970 passengers and 170 standard vehicles. **Service speed** is 19 knots. There are 10 2-berth cabins and 71 4-berth cabins, including 5 deluxe units with sitting rooms. Food service, a cocktail lounge, and a solarium are available. Crew of 64 is required on board.

LeConte was launched in late 1973 by Peterson Shipbuilders in Sturgeon Bay, Wisconsin, and joined the Alaska Marine Highway fleet in 1974. **Length** is 235 feet, **beam** is 57 feet, **draft** is 12 feet 9 inches, and **horsepower** is 4,300 with capacity for 250 passengers and 47standard vehicles. **Service speed** is 14 knots. Food service, a cocktail lounge, and a solarium are provided. A crew of 24 is required on board.

Malaspina was built in Seattle, Washington, in 1963 at the Lockheed Shipbuilding yards, then lengthened and renovated in 1972 at the Willamette Iron and Steel Company shipyard in Portland, Oregon. **Length** is 408 feet, **beam** is 74 feet, **draft** is 15 feet, **horse-power** is 8,000. She carries 750 passengers and 120 standard vehicles. **Service speed** is 16.5 knots. There are 56 4-berth and 30 2-berth cabins. Food service, a cocktail lounge, and a solarium are available. Crew of 58 is required on board.

Matanuska was built by Puget Sound Bridge & Dry Dock Company of Seattle, Washington,and began service in 1963. In 1978, she was lengthened and renovated. **Length** is 408 feet, **beam** is 74 feet, **draft** is 15 feet, **horsepower** is 8,000, with capacity for 120 standard vehicles and 746 passengers. **Service speed** is 16.5 knots. There are 84 2-berth, 24 3-berth, and 4 4-berth cabins. Food service, a cocktail lounge, and a solarium are provided. A crew of 58 is required on board.

Taku was built by Puget Sound Bridge & Dry Dock Company of Seattle,Washington,and began service in 1963. **Length** is 352 feet, **beam** is 74 feet, **draft** is 15 feet, **horsepower** is 8,000, with capacity for 105 standard vehicles, and a passenger capacity of 500. **Service speed** is 16 knots. She was renovated in 1981, and has 35 2-berth and 9 4-berth cabins. Food service, a cocktail lounge, and a solarium are available. A crew of 42 is required on board.

Tustumena known as the "Trusty Tusty," is the fleet's only ocean licensed vessel and serves the Kenai Peninsula. Her home port is Seward. Built at Sturgeon Bay, Wisconsin, in 1964, she sailed in Alaskan waters for five years, then was renovated in San Francisco in the winter of 1969. **Length** is 296 feet, **beam** is 59 feet, **draft** is 15 feet, **horsepower** is 3,600, with space for 50 standard vehicles and a passenger capacity of 325. **Service speed** is 14 knots. There are 25 2-berth and 2 4-berth cabins. Food service, a cocktail lounge, and a solarium are available. Crew of 37 is required on board.

Anisim Kalugin, Age 12, Sixth Grade, Nikolaevsk School (Anchor Point)